OUTDOOR
LIVING

KAREN ROOS
ANNEMARIE MEINTJES

OUTDOOR LIVING

PHOTOGRAPHY
MASSIMO CECCONI

TEXT
LAURIAN BROWN

contents

introduction 6

room outside 8
opening the indoors
to the outdoors

solitude 30
open-air sanctuaries
and retreats

company 38
getting together outdoors

entertaining 62
setting the party scene

the kitchen garden 72
fresh delights from pot
or potager

the potted garden 84
contained pleasures

connections 96
moments in space
and time

the elements 106
painting the picture

texture and pattern 106
plants 118
water 132

database 140

introduction

Step outside and the clock slows. Time spent out of doors is time won, restorative breathing space in an increasingly pressured world.

Now, more than ever, every home needs a room beyond its four walls, entirely removed from technology. Wherever you live, it's possible to create such a space, roofed by the sky or open to a garden, where you can reconnect with yourself and the natural world. It may also be a place to reconnect with family and friends, for companionable relaxation or entertaining. It may be a flat balcony, a courtyard, a modern deck, a rooftop, an old-fashioned stoep or a corner of the garden.

The idea of the outdoor room is as old as gardening itself, but this is not a gardening book. It draws on the best of traditional and modern examples to show you how to transform the space available to you into a magical retreat. It's about defining that space and establishing atmosphere with sunlight and shadow, texture and pattern, furniture and plants. It's about quiet moments, simple pleasures and designs both grand and humble. Many of the ideas may be translated from large to small spaces, and vice versa.

These inspired and inspiring outdoor spaces were photographed in South Africa, but the trends are universal.

FAR LEFT AND LEFT
Beginning at the beginning: two very different but equally inviting entrances make the transition from public to private space an intriguing, unwinding moment for visitors.

room outside

Opening out is something South Africans love to do, have to do. The climate makes it irresistible, if not compulsory, to change windows into doors. For every kind of dwelling, this mindset offers a potential extension of living space. At its most basic, this may be a simple terrace open to the sky or the deep shelter of a traditional stoep. In contemporary confines, the high-walled privacy of a courtyard or the simple breathing space of a flat balcony gives the city dweller that vital 'extra room' outdoors.

LEFT
Upstairs space need not be confined. At Auberge Clermont guesthouse in the Boland, this bedroom opens charmingly onto a small balcony, enclosed in glass to provide protection from the Cape winds. Lilac-painted wooden stairs extend the access to the garden.

The traditional South African stoep is perhaps the most perfect link between indoors and out, ideal for entertaining, quiet contemplation or simple daydreaming. It provides shelter in most weathers; depending on the season, it's a place both to escape from or to seek the sun. On the north side of a house, it's a cool retreat in summer, a suntrap in the winter.

On the west, a stoep is completely essential: one, to screen the house from the fierce rays of summer afternoons, and two, to watch the sunset.

RIGHT
A new generation has rediscovered the practical virtues and comforts of the stoep, building houses graced with the deep pillared verandahs of yesteryear – and with them, something of the drenching peace of long-ago summer afternoons. At La Grange in Franschhoek, nostalgic furnishings such as these Lloyd Loom chairs – in subtly updated colourings – as well as great-grandmother's cascading ferns, geraniums and begonias enhance the mood.

FOLLOWING PAGE
A wide, oak-lined verandah provides cool shelter for the clubhouse at Domaine des Anges, an innovative housing development in Franschhoek.

ROOM OUTSIDE | 13

PREVIOUS PAGE LEFT
Sunny stoeps need cool colour schemes. Hardy Mediterranean herbs and succulents make ideal container plants for sunbaked aspects and contribute a refreshing and fragrant blue note to the setting.

PREVIOUS PAGE RIGHT
White and green cool the long stoep of a restored colonial house in Cape Town. French doors and white louvred shutters open onto a screed floor coloured with green oxide and green wax polish. The furniture, all compact, light and airy, has been carefully selected to utilise the entire length of the stoep without cluttering it. Lloyd Loom benches and traditional garden chairs and tables positioned between the doors make the most of the long narrow space, elegantly and effectively.

LEFT
For a special, uniquely relaxed ambience, treat outdoor spaces like indoor rooms, using solid, properly cushioned wood furniture instead of garden plastic. Enclosed on three sides by indoor living space, this stoep is furnished with indoor pieces, old and new, to create a stylishly comfortable extension to the surrounding rooms, which open onto it through double glass doors.

ABOVE
Carefully furnished and decorated, a miniscule balcony becomes a delightful open-air retreat. Flags make festive awnings, while old trophies add a sporty note and make 'taking the air' a thoroughly smart occasion.

Balconies and upstairs verandahs have a particular charm. They may be only one or dozens of stories up. Whatever their size, this sense of elevation and airiness should be exploited to the full.

RIGHT

Green plastic and stainless steel furniture suit this modern terrace balcony and its verdant treetop view. Ornamental grasses in galvanised pots are thoroughly contemporary, and also link the balcony to the surrounding urban forest.

PREVIOUS PAGE LEFT

Perched high above Cape Town's city bowl, this Victorian house has one of the most breathtaking views in South Africa, nowhere better enjoyed than on the lacy upstairs verandah, where a narrow table and French café chairs have been neatly slotted into the narrow span to make an enviable alfresco eyrie.

PREVIOUS PAGE RIGHT

Tiled floors and iron pillars are essentially Victorian, but the simplest verandah can be given a period feel, not by tacking on 'broekie lace', but rather by adding hanging baskets and plants in pretty stands. Filled with chocolate-leaf pelargoniums, this beautiful potstand of French wirework is a replica of a period design and forms both a screen and a focal point when viewed from indoors.

Courtyards are among the most ancient of outdoor rooms. The cool water-lit atriums of the Romans and the creeper-hung courtyards of the Moors provide perfect inspiration for the modern townhouse dweller. At this studio flat the simplest elements combine to make tranquil magic: cobble paving edged with klompjes frames a rill flowing into a classic pond. Planting is minimal: terracotta pots brimming with oxalis and orange trees, which will grow to form a solid wall of green.

Colour plays a vital and magic role in adding atmosphere to enclosed spaces, particularly those with high walls or double-storeyed surrounds. Classic ochre or terracotta would be safe options, but these daring pink walls transform a potentially gloomy courtyard into an upbeat, inviting space.

PREVIOUS PAGES

Large subtropical plants in small spaces create drama and a real sense of escape. Normally tender plants will also flourish in the shelter provided by a walled enclosure, creating their own jungle microclimate. This small city courtyard has been transformed by bold, overscaled planting on different levels, enhanced by careful choice of evocative accessories and furnishings like the Indian daybed.

ABOVE

Any flat roof has potential as an outdoor room – provided access can be comfortably contrived. This opulent hideaway was conjured on bare, strictly functional architecture by imaginative and extravagant furnishing. Oversized pieces, rich fabrics, dark polished woods and palms planted in handsome, round-bellied pots have reinvented this space completely.

RIGHT

Behind the parapet of a flat roof, a hidden retreat has been created chiefly by finishing the surface simply and elegantly. A screed, coloured with red oxide, makes an attractive waterproof floor. Minimal furnishing – an old cast iron birdbath and traditional wood and metal bench – make it a place for quiet early mornings and sundown moments.

solitude

For stressed city dwellers, fresh air and green peace have become vital restoratives. Every garden, every soul, needs a place of peace and privacy, somewhere to relax away from the computer coalface, where we can reconnect with the natural world. It could be a wild and leafy place, or surrounded by sky – a rock, a terrace, even a treehouse. Or it could be a secluded corner of simple Zen-like calm. It may require planning, planting, building, or no more than the placing of a bench or chair.

LEFT
A small forest of birches in a city garden provides a wild and restful setting for a simple stone bench. Natural plantings of deciduous trees and groundcovers such as this not only mark the changing of the seasons, but also create a haven for birds and insects, as well as a green sanctuary for the city-pent.

RIGHT

In cities, particularly in high-density housing estates and complexes, walls and trees provide vital seclusion and a sense of sanctuary. In this townhouse courtyard an old fig tree spared by the builders has become the focal point of a small urban jungle. Every effort should be made to spare trees on site during building operations. Mature trees, their branches sculpted by time, are themselves symbols of sanctuary, especially in Africa, and the most valuable asset any new garden can have. Here, the dense planting of tall, bold-leaved plants conceals the shape and boundaries of what is essentially a small, square space and heightens the wonderful fantasy of this retreat.

FOLLOWING PAGE LEFT

A hammock, a charming symbol of absolute leisure, supplies the same marvellous sense of airy suspension in a world of dappled light and shade. It also provides an inviting focal point and is a useful reminder of the need for relaxation.

FOLLOWING PAGE RIGHT

The ultimate outdoor retreat defies gravity, elevating you into an airy, leafy world of birds and insects. This tree house, high up in the branches of an oak tree, provides an adventurous escape for a child or adult.

ABOVE

The pleasure of outdoor privacy is nowhere better enjoyed than in an open-air shower. There's nothing easier to devise either. Here, rough poles and bamboo screens create a rustic retreat.

RIGHT

Around the lichen-painted trunks of indigenous blue guarries *(Euclea crispa)*, a loose, deep planting of *fluitjiesriet (Phragmites australis)* has created a Zen-like sanctuary. Clay pots provide a sculptural focus; the vertical patterns of the reeds, echoed by the lines of sleepers set in the sand, establish a powerful visual calm. Cool shade, dappled light, the canopy of trees and encircling reeds combine to create a murmuring peace and a sense of airy enclosure.

company

Getting together outdoors is one of South Africa's most pleasant traditions. For generations, *alfresco* meant the stoep, the summerhouse, or simply the shade of the garden's largest tree. From the 1960s, however, nearly every garden had to have a swimming pool, and this alluring stretch of aquamarine became our favourite meeting and relaxing place.

We've come a long way from those bright squares and kidney shapes and their sunbaked surrounds, but water remains a magnet. Superbly designed hotel pools have inspired a new generation of home builders to integrate their pools into the garden and the landscape, to compelling and romantic effect.

LEFT
Designed to exploit its magnificent site on a rocky ridge overlooking Johannesburg's northern suburbs, the beautiful curve of this pool merges with the sky.

Environmental concerns and modern stress have combined to inspire a new naturalism in garden and pool design. City-dwelling South Africans are more nostalgic than ever about the bush, striving to recreate a slice of the wild to come home to every evening after a hard, technology-driven day. We want to feel we're taking a dip in the Blyde River or even a farm dam, rather than an Olympic-style bath of improbable turquoise. Shapes may be formal or naturalistic, but the colour of the water is always keyed to the setting. Painting the interior of the pool dark blue, grey, black or a sand colour makes all the difference, transforming the water into a mountain stream, a rock pool or even a drop of the ocean.

RIGHT

A round plunge pool can be formal or organic and takes up little space. At this house in the old Johannesburg suburb of Westcliff the indigenous bush has been retained and enhanced to provide a harmonious setting for the African style of the architecture (see overleaf). The brimming pool has been integrated into a series of decks that extend the living spaces of the house into its wild setting. Raised via a stone wall to the lower deck level, the structure is reminiscent of farm dams, favourite swimming places of country childhoods. It functions as both pool and conversation pit; the perfect place to cool off at the end of a high-powered day. A rustic bench and an antique Balinese recliner link the outdoors to the indoor style of the house.

LEFT AND RIGHT

Indoors and out merge into one another via glass walls and floors that flow out into decking. Trees on the site have been integrated into the structure, rather than felled. The organic style of the architecture weaves together texture, form and pattern into a charming and fantastical environment. Indoors and out, primitive craft pieces from both Africa and the East provide a whimsical and harmonious decorative note.

FOLLOWING PAGES

In an architectural setting of Japanese simplicity, outdoor dining has an ocean view; a rectangular plunge pool provides a small mirror of the sky.

The warmth and comfort of wood underfoot and its lightness of construction has made it a popular material for pool surrounds as well as the building of extra outdoor living space. Moroccan grass beds make pleasingly natural recliners.

PREVIOUS PAGE RIGHT
Sheltered by the house, which surrounds it on three sides, the shape of this pool is not only an inspired element in the whole design, but it also leads the eye like a river towards the Atlantic Ocean. Shaded by the shapely branches of old stone pines, the terrace and dining areas command a mesmerising view of the sea.

ABOVE
Timber walls, bleached pastel wooden furniture and piles of sea-scoured pebbles enhance the time-out mood.

RIGHT
With direct access to the beach, this elegantly casual house has a distinctly ocean-going feel about it. The balustrades of upper and lower decks are made of steel cable, while a canvas awning provides overhead shade. The repeated patterns of parallel lines make for tranquillity, the use of plain, light, airy materials and colours spell holiday.

In a highly successful integration of the indoors and the outdoors, balconies, gazebos and terraces open out and look down onto a lap pool that runs almost the entire length of this Oranjezicht house. The play of different levels and views makes dramatic and maximum use of the steeply sloping, heavily treed site.

Outdoor living spaces need to be furnished as carefully as indoor rooms. Furnishing and accessories should be chosen to harmonise with, and enhance, the architectural forms and the planting. For complete continuity, the interior style and colours of the house itself should also be taken into consideration. This applies to old houses as well as ultra-modern ones, but is especially important in those with an open interface or good flow between indoors and out. Even views from windows should have some visual link with that specific room. Colour is particularly important here. Tying the planting outside to the colour scheme of the room can make a dramatic difference to the charm of both.

The plastic chair has been reinvented: explore the range of witty and stylish designs now available. Use paint to revitalise old wroughtiron, 1950s mesh or wood; once again colour can link odd or incongruous pieces of furniture and their setting into a harmonious whole.

LEFT
The elegant curve of this Deco-style pool is perfectly complemented by its immaculately tiled surrounds, as well as the clean bow of the recliner alongside.

Traditional architecture demands a traditional pool, opulent recliners and a blue to match the ocean beyond. Ellerman House in Bantry Bay, once the home of shipping magnate Sir John Ellerman, has been restored and converted into a luxury guest house. The elaborate arches and balustrades of the old mansion called for a simple rectangular pool of generous proportions. Sited on the broad terrace below the main house, it has been designed as an extension of the whole structure, and is linked to it by a handsomely proportioned pergola. The festive pink stripes of the chairs echo the paler Bahamas pink of the house itself. The immaculate lawns around it are shaded by palms and eucalyptus of the old garden and scented by frangipani.

LEFT

The starkly sculpted trunk of a eucalyptus tree sets the style for this rustic pool, bordered with rocks, rough logs for seating and screened by pole fencing. It's a dramatic Wild West treatment entirely in keeping with its rural Hout Bay setting and the magnificent surroundings reflected in its limpid waters.

FOLLOWING PAGE

There are many ways to fit the pool to the setting. The classic scroll of this fountain feeds a semicircular shell, the elegant proportions of which nod quietly to its historic Cape context. The formality of the design is surprisingly well offset by its backdrop of farmland and countryside. A newly planted avenue of young conifers behind the pool promises future enhancement.

LEFT

The pool at Saint Verde in KwaZulu-Natal is practical and beautiful in its farmyard setting. The base has been painted black both to retain heat and reflect the verdant surroundings. Stone Chinese lions at each corner lend a long-established air, but are only about five years old. Square flagstones – set edge to edge and point to point – are among the most attractive and simple paving materials available. Interspersed with pebbles and groundcovers, they create a restful yet interesting tapestry around the water and in no way complicate or distract from the charm of the dry-stone wall which underlines the trees and hills beyond.

entertaining

Outdoors, South Africans have always been a nation of picnickers and lap diners. Now we've discovered the charm of the formally laid table under the stars.

Even in our splendid climate, it's a case of 'weather permitting'. A permanent outdoor dining area, close to the kitchen, cool in the day, balmy at night, is the best solution. But the moveable feast also has its own magic. With a folding table and light chairs you can set up your banquet to make the most of the day, the garden and the season: under a tree in blossom, out on the deck, wherever the shade is coolest and deepest, or simply out of the wind.

LEFT
Fresh air, fresh fruit, dessert wine: with your best china and silver, the simplest outdoor meal becomes a banquet. A cloth is not obligatory, unless you need to hide the table top.

Most city gardeners strive to create a mood of fantasy in their plots and 'pocket handkerchiefs'. Garden parties can capitalise on this, using furniture and table settings that create an exotic or rustic atmosphere. Plan the menu to match.

RIGHT

Completely sheltered from all weather vagaries except rain, this lushly-planted courtyard has a distinctly Moorish feel. The supper party setting is appropriately Moroccan: velvet upholstered carvers have been brought from indoors, sumptuous cushions dress up rustic benches, not only for effect but also because comfortable, stable seating is vital to the success of any dinner party. The handsome table has been laid with simple table mats and festively crowded with capacious glasses, ornate silver and antique brass.

FOLLOWING PAGE

You can set up shade wherever you want it in the garden with this simple, overhead awning. Four sapling poles and a piece of fabric may be anchored anywhere to create an atmospheric outdoor room. Although lightweight fabric is easier to handle, it will not provide as much shade as heavier fabric like canvas. For complete stability, guyropes are a good idea.

A charming provincial table and odd garden and folding chairs create a robust expectation of the best of country fare to come.

ABOVE

Old walls create an extraordinary ambience: instead of being restored, this old stable wall has been exposed to show the layering of centuries. The placing (in sufficiently sheltered spots) of indoor rather than garden furniture, such as this table, adds mood and depth.

RIGHT

This old-world space, with its weathered walls and cobbled paving, calls for the simplest of settings. For a formal meal, the table is draped in an old, heavy linen cloth, while plain white plates and antique glasses are set around a central candlestick placed on a circle of fig leaves – the only decorative touch.

FOLLOWING PAGES

Observe your garden for good dining-out spots through the seasons. Spectacular or fragrant seasonal flowering – such as orange or lemon blossoming, wisteria, or moonflower – provide both a reason and a setting for a celebration. Simply laying a table in any green or wild spot in the garden on a balmy evening will create a sense of occasion. Tealights provide the most inexpensive lighting solution and are available in mosquito-repellent citronella, a precaution vital to the comfort and enjoyment of evenings outdoors.

the kitchen garden

Two of the favourite pastimes of the new millennium have become virtually inseparable. No kitchen should be without its own garden now. Growing your own can make all the difference to the kind of food you serve – and add enormously to the pleasure of cooking. Even the smallest patch can supply the ambitious cook with fresh herbs and salad greens, as well as vital flavours and textures to enhance the simplest meal.

There are many ways and places to be a gourmet gardener; aim for a patch that brims with promise and produces neither too much nor too little for your table and your friends.

LEFT
In orderly rows or tucked among the flowers, vegetables have a beauty of their own. With silvery fretwork leaves and sculptured buds and flowers, Globe artichokes are among the handsomest of gourmet plants.

Vegetables need plenty of light and at least six hours of sunlight a day, so site your patch accordingly. Where space is limited, concentrate on growing only what is best, or what you love but can't easily buy. Herbs and salad greens such as looseleaf lettuces, rocket, sorrel and chives are good first choices. In small spaces or gardens where the light changes dramatically with the seasons, moveable wooden tubs or barrels can support an adequate supply of these herbs and greens all year round.

RIGHT
The kitchen of this apartment looks out onto a narrow but abundant *potager*, an appetising view for both cook and guest. Rows of lush tatsoi and spring onions cater to the cook's Oriental bias.

FOLLOWING PAGE LEFT
In this newly planted herb garden, a chequerboard of pennyroyal and thyme interspersed with pebbles follows the curve of an old wall. Welded steel bands sunk 20 cm into the beds keep the plants, the pebbles and the pattern in place.

FOLLOWING PAGE RIGHT
Not strictly a kitchen garden, but definitely one to brighten the cook's life, this sink looks out onto a narrow alley which receives no more than two hours of sunlight a day. Although not enough for herbs or vegetables, it is plenty of light for tough shade-lovers like these *Sansevieras*, planted here in terracotta pots set in wall rings.

ABOVE AND RIGHT

There are many styles of traditional kitchen garden: simple, elaborate or cottagey. This one of raised beds, supported by pressure-treated saplings, harks back to medieval monastery gardens. It's an attractive, rustic system that makes not only for easier soil preparation and excellent drainage, but also for easier planting and picking. Wedge-shaped beds, arranged around a central paved circle, contain mixed yet orderly plantings of vegetables and cascades of herbs. The beds are narrow enough to allow access from the sides to the centre. Avoid stepping on prepared soil as it will cause compaction.

Even the smallest space, provided it has good light and at least six hours of sun, can produce vegetables in season for the dedicated cook. An inspiring range of gourmet roots, leaves and baby vegetables is now available, which makes productive container gardening much easier.

THE KITCHEN GARDEN

PREVIOUS PAGE LEFT

Many vegetables can be grown successfully in containers provided they are given adequate depth of soil and are fed regularly. In this narrow lane scarlet runner beans in old cement pots climb up tripods to provide a decorative and nutritious note of green; an excellent solution for small spaces.

PREVIOUS PAGE RIGHT

A formal vegetable garden, sited on a terrace below this Johannesburg house, provides an inviting view from the deck above.

RIGHT

Designed with the view from the house in mind, this formal herb garden of concentric squares and playfully staggered patterns combines low, clipped hedging with natural plant forms.

the potted garden

Containers are breathtakingly liberating. As living space contracts, more and more South African gardeners are discovering the freedom of this type of gardening. You decide what to grow and where to grow it. Each precious plant can enjoy the right soil, the right amount of water, the right amount of light. And when you move, your garden moves with you.

If you're a decorator rather than a gardener, pots are for you. They set the mood and can transform the bleakest outdoor space. Two grand urns with citrus trees can turn a backyard into Tuscany. Fifty simple pots, large and small, create a jungle.

LEFT
Container planting at its best highlights the form and individuality of plants. Raised and isolated in an island of pebbles, the stark beauty of *Aloe dichotoma* creates a dramatic focus and brings the sky and space of Bushmanland to this KwaZulu-Natal garden.

ABOVE

Containers are essentially statuary. Nowhere is this better expressed than in the art of sculptor and potter Dina Prinsloo, and her art lies in perfectly matching container to plant. At the entrance to her Johannesburg home, a wall bay frames a group of living sculptures.

RIGHT

Dina's greenhouse holds her working material, a vast collection of plants chosen for their striking forms and growth habits. Along the path outside, the sunlovers are ranged in a rich and fascinating composition of clay and plant material.

PREVIOUS PAGE

Inside Dina Prinsloo's greenhouse, light filters through a roof of saplings onto shade-loving plants in simple pots – a fascinating testimony to the variety and individuality to be found in the green world. The quiet energy of a plant house or collection like this creates a marvellously restorative ambience for a city retreat.

LEFT

In the courtyard, a series of small sculptures set in coarse gravel are grouped to form a larger work.

CENTRE

In faultless harmony of plant and clay, one sculpture grows out of another. Form, habitat, and plant colour all combine to influence the final design.

RIGHT

Tall cylindrical pots make a perfect home for low plantings of cacti. They add strength to the picture while integrating perfectly into the forms and patterns of the garden.

CLOCKWISE FROM LOWER RIGHT: Raised wooden boxes planted with clumps of *Festuca glauca* make a graphic addition to a seaside deck (see also page 42); conifers are thoroughly at home in traditional whitewashed concrete dressed with pebbles; black pansies make striking pot subjects; a combination of a large grey, glazed pot and tiny terracotta pots hold dark red leaves of peppermint and cabbage

on a table improvised from concrete balustrades; the rough texture of this charmingly distressed pot offsets the leaves and flowers of the slipper plant (*Calceolaria crenatiflora*); silvery herbs look good in weathered tin; classic terracotta pots of every size remain a best basic.

Square galvanised pots planted with silvery blue *Festuca glauca* grass make an elegant cubist trio.

Materials, scale and tradition combine to make wooden half barrels the perfect container for Cape Dutch-style exteriors.

Paired topiaries make entrances inviting and hint at charm within. Evergreen foliage can look very good in pots of similar colour and sheen – twin clipped *Eugenia myrtifolia* **in green-glazed French Onduze pots lend grace and whimsy to this doorway.**

connections

We connect to the infinite via the finite and our appreciation of outdoor space is hugely enhanced by the way we frame or measure it. In the veld, we need a single koppie, a solitary tree, a cloud, something of a scale we can read, as a measure and a link to the vastness around us. In our own restricted outdoor spaces a similar principle applies; how we define that space makes the connection and the magic. We can frame the view beyond or within; we can play with scale and so enlarge or contract it. Arches, arbours and ornaments are only some of the many connecting devices we can use to link us to a wider view. They can also work by reverse association, creating a sense of the infinite in an all too finite space.

LEFT
In small spaces, a simple sculptural device can create a sense of distance and make oppressive walls recede. Here a square pillar – one of a group of three – topped with a sphere, brings air and depth to a Sandton courtyard.

THIS AND PREVIOUS PAGES

In spaces both large and small an arch remains one of the most effective and romantic connecting devices. It may form an inviting link between one space and another, create or enhance a view within or provide dramatic measure of the view beyond. Traditionally draped with fragrant climbers, it enforces a cool, delicious pause.

LEFT

In small courtyards the enclosing walls provide a frame for the sky that may be enhanced playfully or dramatically by the architecture. In this entrance court, the deep shadow of the arch below the outside staircase presents a cool contrast to the sunbaked walls and blue sky, to which the eye is led upwards by the steady march of the steps and the pots.

CENTRE

The dark, cool confines of a narrow, high-walled entrance contrast with the sunlit upper storey glimpsed ahead, impelling the visitor forward to the intriguing, lighter space beyond. The play of angles and volumes is reflected in the detail of square windows and sculpted pots.

RIGHT

Once again steps lead the eye upward to a group of sculpted containers, a simple yet powerful linking device between inside and beyond, earth and sky. The rich soft terracotta of the walls was achieved by mixing the plaster with red riversand. According to the colour and source of the sand, the colour of the plaster may vary from biscuit to many shades of ochre – a much more natural and satisfying finish than paint can provide.

FOLLOWING PAGES FROM LEFT TO RIGHT

Connecting with garden tradition and time: a collection of old watering cans makes a focal point; a single round window in a creeper-clad city wall sets the imagination free; connecting worlds: seated on a lavender hedge, a small Buddha holds a bouquet of purple plastic roses.

the elements
texture and pattern

There's much more to the gardener's palette than plants. Sunlight and shadow, paving, walling, water, and various natural and industrial forms and textures all help to define space and establish atmosphere and interest.

Building and paving materials play a major role in a garden's style and atmosphere. For example, hard-edged paving and face-brick walls strike a harsh industrial note that demands considerable effort and planting to soften and mellow. Old stock brick, stone, wood and gravel, even in stark and minimal designs, create a more sympathetic mood. A sharpened appreciation and enjoyment of simple natural forms and textures – bark, twisted stems, weathered wood, moss and pebbles – has promoted their use in gardens.

LEFT
Shells, instead of pebbles, add an evocative marine note. Best in simple settings with formal stone or rustic driftwood, here they cover a wall, but a smaller collection might be placed in a stone basin and set among grey-leaved plants.

Walls need not be cloaked with plants. They can also be used as a canvas for changing patterns of sunlight and shadow through the day. Plants alone may paint an interesting picture, but a combination of structural organic elements can add another dimension, framing and highlighting their signature.

RIGHT

In this entrance court only wood is used, creating an abstract interplay of growing and structural forms. A pergola combines with the walls to define the space, both vertically and horizontally. The shapes of treetrunks are framed by poles, which repeat their colour and texture, and link the house to the garden via the use of the same material.

FOLLOWING PAGE LEFT

In an old-fashioned *werf* of raked earth, the deeply fissured trunks of *Erythrina latissima* form a striking sculpture, offset by a black-painted door. Piles of rough quartz create an interesting pediment as well as a water reservoir.

FOLLOWING PAGE RIGHT

Inspired by the kraals of the Pedi and other northern tribes, this rustic screen of mopani wood adds a slice of the wild to a Saxonwold garden.

Architects, designers and gardeners are retreating from European models, to traditional South African rustic styles. Raked or stamped earth, handbuilt kraal and reed fences, instead of lawn and prim pickets, are an evocative foil for the sculpture of indigenous plants.

ABOVE
Traditional construction methods and materials impart solidity, strength and charm. This wooden farm loft with a packed stone wall was built to house mountain goats, and is a model of rustic excellence. It features contrasting patterns and equally rugged textures.

RIGHT
On a different scale, but exploiting a similar combination, this pool paving made of rough-hewn, heavily weathered sleepers edged with pebbles adds earthy strength and substance to a city courtyard.

Surplus stone in the garden can almost always be put to good use. Stockpile it rather than pay to have it carted away. Small stones can be used both practically and decoratively, for paving, drainage channels, reservoirs or mulch. If you have enough large stone, a section of dry wall, even as a retainer or a focal point, makes a marvellous feature in almost any style of garden. Even in cities, stone masons can still be found who know how to pack such walls.

Stone and wood may be combined effectively on different scales and in many different ways.

LEFT AND FAR RIGHT

In this striking fountain, old and new, rough and smooth, are combined in an abstract that changes constantly with the movement of sun and water. Eighteenth century Flemish waterspouts set in *hartsteen* spill water into a bowl cut from Table Mountain granite. From there water overflows into a pond edged in polished granite. Beneath its surface, river pebbles add light, texture and pattern.

ABOVE AND RIGHT

Wooden decking is a versatile material, which in spite of its immaculate machined construction, can be given different finishes to suit its setting. Balau is the recommended wood: this design has been given an edging of studs, smoothly picoted and treated with a matt varnish to help it retain its rich colour. The finish and patterns complement the style of the house, the pool and the wild setting.

FOLLOWING PAGE LEFT

Old bricks softened with moss convey an age and mellowness that may simply be due to a cool, damp aspect. Moss grows more easily on rough, porous surfaces such as that of stock brick. Encourage it with regular spraying down with water or a weak solution of liquid fertiliser. Painting with yoghurt works well on statuary and pots.

FOLLOWING PAGE RIGHT

Mixed recycled materials can be used to exciting effect. In the mood of Helen Martins and The Owl House, glass, broken tiles and crockery can be set in cement, on walls and in paths to create a splash or a whole world of light and colour.

the elements
plants

Plants play a vital role in establishing the mood of your outdoor space. Together with your architecture, they represent your basic design and building materials. Plants build atmosphere not only by association, but also by their shapes, patterns and colours, the ways in which they catch light and cast shadows. A dark, dense backdrop of evergreens will give your space a sense of secret enclosure; a light-leaved, silvery planting, a sense of sun and warmth, and open country.

CLOCKWISE FROM TOP LEFT
Cacti bring big sky and wide horizons; clipped lavender slows the clock to *Provençal* time; roses suggest country house romance or cottage splendour; palms rustle in the tropics.

ABOVE AND RIGHT

Once Upon a Time in the West: In a witty mix of formal and desert gardening, a succulent collection brings Arizona and the widest of open spaces to the green Midlands of KwaZulu-Natal.

Isolated in raised beds and spaced out in perfect compositions in their own mini-desert, the stark forms of the succulents are in harmony with the pioneer style of the farmhouse. Scattered bones and raking light echo the covers of a thousand pulp Westerns.

Each plant's shape and texture is a reflection of its natural environment and the prevailing conditions. Felty, grey and feathery leaves are adaptations for full sun and hot dry conditions; dark green and shiny leaves usually seek shade. The bigger the leaf, the more water the plant will probably want. With these characteristics come associations as well as aura. Plants are highly evocative. With them they bring jungle, desert, mountain, kloof, veld – Brazil, Sante Fé, Thabazimbi, St Tropez.

LEFT

Succulents are not only the most evolved, but also among the most fascinating of plants. Gravel beds, raised for good drainage, display their unique and richly varied forms to excellent advantage. Predominant leaf colour is sun-defying grey, damask-smooth or grainy, powdery here, lacquered there, and lit with jade or turquoise.

RIGHT

For a sense of age and place, add a dry stone wall, a natural environment for succulents, alpine plants and geckos. Depending on the planting, it may spell Provence, Mexico, Europe or Africa.

FOLLOWING PAGE

When plants are allowed a free hand within a formal structure, the results have a charming air of secluded exuberance. At Saint Verde in KwaZulu-Natal, this gate of French wirework draws its ordered filigree across an Impressionist cloud of colour that tumbles over paving and spills from pots of different sizes.

Plants may also be manipulated to equally beguiling effect. This sculpted garden with its clipped lavender bushes, bay trees and silvery olives, brings the textures and colours of Provence to Franschhoek and is in perfect harmony with both house and setting.

LEFT

This stretch of ecru wall has been capped with a gable of packed stones – an effective sculpture as well as a security device. Throughout the garden, walls are underlined and softened with low hedges of *Eugenia myrtifolia*. Young bay and citrus trees will grow up to cloak the plaster in varying shades of green.

ABOVE

Clipping and topiary not only create attractive forms and patterns but also suggest a world of unlimited time, where infinite care may be taken over elegant whimsy.

FOLLOWING PAGE

In this formal Johannesburg garden, low walls, clipped hedges and statuary are offset by a riot of roses, curtains of old creepers and a backdrop of mature trees.

the elements
water

Because our most basic instincts are so tuned to seek out this most precious of elements, its presence unfailingly reassures and exhilarates us. Water has always been a vital resource in gardens, not only for the nurture of plants and creatures, but for its ability to soothe and entrance. A water feature brings life into any outdoor space via sound, sparkle, reflection, birds and insects. Wide, still pools work especially well in broad, open gardens, reflecting the surrounding scene and the clouds above. In gloomy city courtyards, even something as small as a birdbath will bring the sky down into the garden.

LEFT
The sound of falling water is both alluring and cooling. In city outdoor spaces, it can help distract from and conceal traffic noise. Fountains may need careful tuning to achieve just the right tone and volume.

In a fundamentally hot and dry country like South Africa, it's important to work sparingly and reverently with water. Here we can learn from the Moors and their inspired and economic deployment of it – to magical effect – in runnels, rills, single jets, dripping waterspouts and shallow reflecting ponds. As a rule, the simpler the water feature, the better, both for effective design and ease of construction and maintenance. Research pays. Pools do not, however, always need filters and pumps. Correctly planted and stocked with fish (not koi, which need highly oxygenated water) such as this pond (right), they can achieve and maintain excellent clarity.

RIGHT

In this traditonal, country-style garden, *waterblommetjies (Aponogeton distachyos)* grow in a simple rectangular raised pond. A broad rim on two sides provides seating, while a row of dwarf orange trees clipped into a hedge, forms a fragrant green backdrop, screening the pond from the potting shed beyond.

A classic pond, set in granite and edged with handmade *klompje* bricks, brings coolness and sparkle to this white-walled courtyard. Twice a day the rill flows from a spring to feed the pond and on again to water the rest of the garden.

ABOVE

Long tried and tested, traditional pond and fountain designs are always worth consideration, but make sure that they suit the scale and style of the house. This stone fountain has been set in a circle of green where it shines against its dark backdrop and also catches the late light.

ABOVE

An old granite basin set among pebbles in a formal square brings light to a shady corner. From spring until autumn, white flowers – arums interplanted with Japanese anemones – provide a luminous frame for this small mirror.

LEFT

In a minimal entrance court, a single jet plays in a raised pond; a sparkling welcome for visitors as well as a refreshing view from indoors.

RIGHT

Old Indian laundry tubs stacked on a slate sill make a simple yet very effective dripping cascade. The same could be done with wooden barrels or – for a more avant-garde effect – colourful petrol or oil drums. Choose a container to suit the backdrop – or make one to match.

database

page 6
architect (left): Johan Slee
(011) 646 9935;
architect (right): Trevor Thorold
(021) 689 2626

pages 8 & 9
Auberge Clermont
(021) 876 3700;
architects: Fred de Kock and Truter
(021) 887 2905

pages 10 & 11
La Grange (021) 876 2155,
(012) 342 3758;
Lloyd Loom chairs, Pelerade
showroom (011) 788 7008

pages 12 & 13
Domaine des Anges
(021) 876 4800;
architect: Chris Lötter
(021) 911 0077;
Bali furniture, Wetherleys
(021) 461 5500

pages 14 &15
architect: Trevor Thorold
(021) 689 2626; Lloyd Loom
benches, Pelerade showroom
(011) 788 7008; Hope Traditional

Garden Furniture
(021) 448 7485,
(021) 905 3069

page 16
architect: Johan Slee
(011) 646 9935

page 17
trophies and flags, House Rules
(011) 788 9200

page 19
French wirework potstand by
Sharon Trickett, Saint Verde
(033234) 4356

page 21
green plastic and steel chairs,
Loft Living (021) 422 0088;
square pots, La Grange
(021) 876 2155,
(012) 342 3758

pages 22 & 23
furniture, Hope Traditional
Garden Furniture
(021) 448 7485,
(021) 905 3069.

pages 24 & 25
architect: James Brummer
(011) 880 1646;
Plascon paint colour 'Lemonade',
code A2-5

pages 26 – 28
furniture, Private Collections
(021) 421 0298

page 29
architect: Trevor Thorold
(021) 689-2626;
bench, Hope Traditional
Garden Furniture
(021) 448 7485

pages 32 & 33
swing, Private Collections
(021) 421 0298

page 34
hammock, Mark Schlesinger
083 2611730

page 35
tree house at Domaine des Anges
(021) 876 4800

OUTDOOR LIVING

page 37
containers, Dina Prinsloo
(011) 791 6604

pages 38 & 39
architect: Johan Slee
(011) 646 9935

pages 40 – 43
architects: Silvio Rech & Lesley
Carstens 082 9009935

pages 45 – 47
grass beds and cushions,
The Moroccan Warehouse
(021) 461 8310

pages 48 – 51
architects: Van der Merwe
Miszewski (021) 423 5829

page 52
architect: Xico Meirelles
(021) 462 0170/1

pages 54 & 55
Ellerman House (021) 439 9182

pages 60 & 61
Saint Verde (033234) 4356

pages 62 & 63
furniture, Private Collections
(021) 421 0298;

accessories, The Moroccan
Warehouse
(021) 461 8310

pages 64 & 65
accessories, The Moroccan
Warehouse
(021) 461 8310

pages 66 & 67
glass bottles with silver,
The Moroccan Warehouse
(021) 461 8310;
antique French glass, Le Brocanteur
(021) 461 6805;
chairs, Hope Traditional Garden
Furniture (021) 448 7485

pages 68 & 69
chairs, Hope Traditional Garden
Furniture (021) 448 7485;
table cloth, Le Brocanteur
(021) 461 6805;
urns with sage plants, La Grange,
Franschhoek (021) 876 2155

pages 70 & 71
Mexican pewter plates, glasses,
soup tureens, Hadeda
(011)788 9859;
French café chair, Hope Traditional
Garden Furniture,
(021) 448 7485;
'Feestafels', House Rules
(011) 788 9200

page 77
terracotta pots by Link Potteries from
garden centres countrywide
(011) 837 4138

page 78 & 79
vegetable and herb garden at Saint
Verde (033234) 4356

page 80
Newport cones, Montebello Design
Centre (021) 686 8494

page 81
designer: Rene Slee
(011) 646 0109

page 83
landscape architect: Patrick Watson
(011) 646 8970

pages 86 – 91
containers, Dina Prinsloo
(011) 791 6604;
architect: Wilhelm Lochner
(021) 424 4214

page 93
galvanised pots, La Grange
(021) 876 2155,
(012) 342 3758

pages 102 & 103
architect: Johan Slee
(011) 646 9935

pages 108–110
sculpture and pottery, Dina
Prinsloo (011) 791 6604;
architect: Wilhelm Lochner
(021) 424 4214

page 112
Saint Verde (033234) 4356

pages 114 & 115
fountain, architect: Trevor Thorold
(021) 689 2626

pages 120 – 123
formal succulent garden at Saint
Verde (033234) 4356;
succulents and cacti, Obesa
Nursery (049) 892 4143

pages 124 & 125
French wirework screen and gate
by Sharon Trickett, Saint Verde
(033234) 4356

page 138
architect: Johan Slee
(011) 646 9935;
landscape architect: De Wet Louw
(012) 346 4933

page 139
fountain at Saint Verde
(033234) 4356;
Indian laundry tubs, La Grange
(021) 876 2155,
(012) 342 3758

Authors' acknowledgements

In addition to the architects and suppliers already listed in the database (page 140), we would also like to thank the following people for their kind welcome into their gardens, as well as their assistance with, and contributions to, this book:

   Carl Bronner, Charlotte Daneel, Annabelle and Robert Desfontaines, Libby de Villiers, Mitch Dolby, Marianne Fassler, Merweline van der Merwe, Joe van Rooyen, Graham Viney, Sonja Zimberlin of Limeline.

Struik Publishers (a division of New Holland Publishing (South Africa) (Pty) Ltd)
Cornelis Struik House
80 McKenzie Street
Cape Town, South Africa

First published in 2001

1 2 3 4 5 6 7 8 9 10

Copyright © in published edition: Struik Publishers 2001

Copyright © in text: Karen Roos and Annemarie Meintjes 2001

Copyright © in photography: Struik Publishers 2001

All rights reserved. No part of this publication may be reproduced, stored in a retrieval system or transmitted in any form or by any means, electronic, mechanical, photocopying, recording or otherwise, without the prior written permission of the copyright owner/s.

Text: Laurian Brown

Publishing manager: Linda de Villiers

Editor: Cecilia Barfield

Designer: Petal Palmer

Design assistant: Natascha Adendorff

Photography: Massimo Cecconi (excluding photograph on pages 24/25: © Alain Proust)

Photographer's assistant: Francesco Sardella

Styling assistant: Doeda Mathidza

Reproduction: Hirt & Carter (Cape) (Pty) Ltd

Printing and binding: Tien Wah Press (Pte) Ltd, Singapore

ISBN 1 86872 567 7